ART MAKING

WITH MoMA

ART MAKING WITH MoMA

20 Activities for Kids
Inspired by Artists at
The Museum of Modern Art

Elizabeth Margulies
and **Cari Frisch**

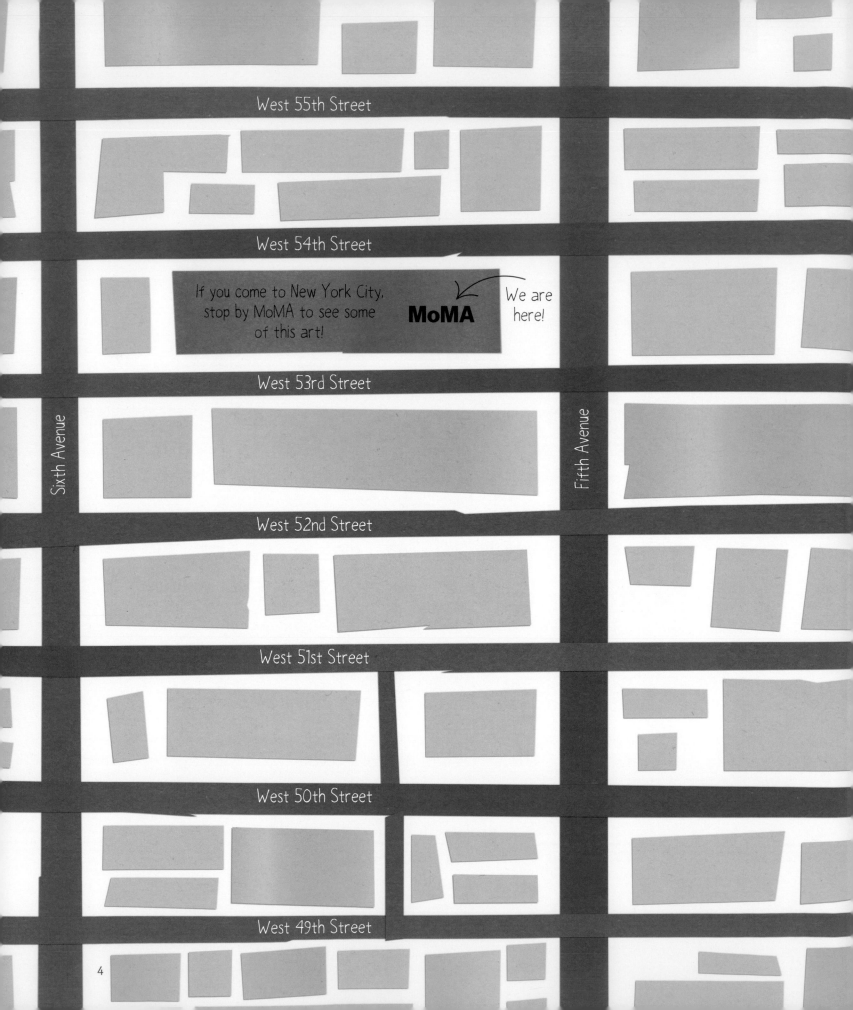

West 55th Street

West 54th Street

If you come to New York City, stop by MoMA to see some of this art!

MoMA

We are here!

West 53rd Street

Sixth Avenue

Fifth Avenue

West 52nd Street

West 51st Street

West 50th Street

West 49th Street

Art Making with MoMA

The activities in this book were inspired by our experiences of looking at and making art with kids and families at The Museum of Modern Art.

MoMA collects and displays art made within the last 150 years—including paintings, sculptures, drawings, prints, photographs, design objects, architectural drawings and models, films, and performances.

At MoMA we encourage kids and adults to discover how modern and contemporary artists experiment with materials and techniques, and to consider how artists respond to the events, people, and places around them.

The instructions, questions, images, and art in this book are just a few different ways to get started. And from there, you can begin to think like an artist, developing your own techniques and discovering new ideas for making art. With this book we hope you will:

Explore

Tinker

Make marks

Combine materials

Design something new

Work together

Change your perspective

Create patterns

Tell your story

Transform yourself into someone else

Make some noise

Listen

Play games

Mix things up

Get messy

Start over

CONTE

NTS

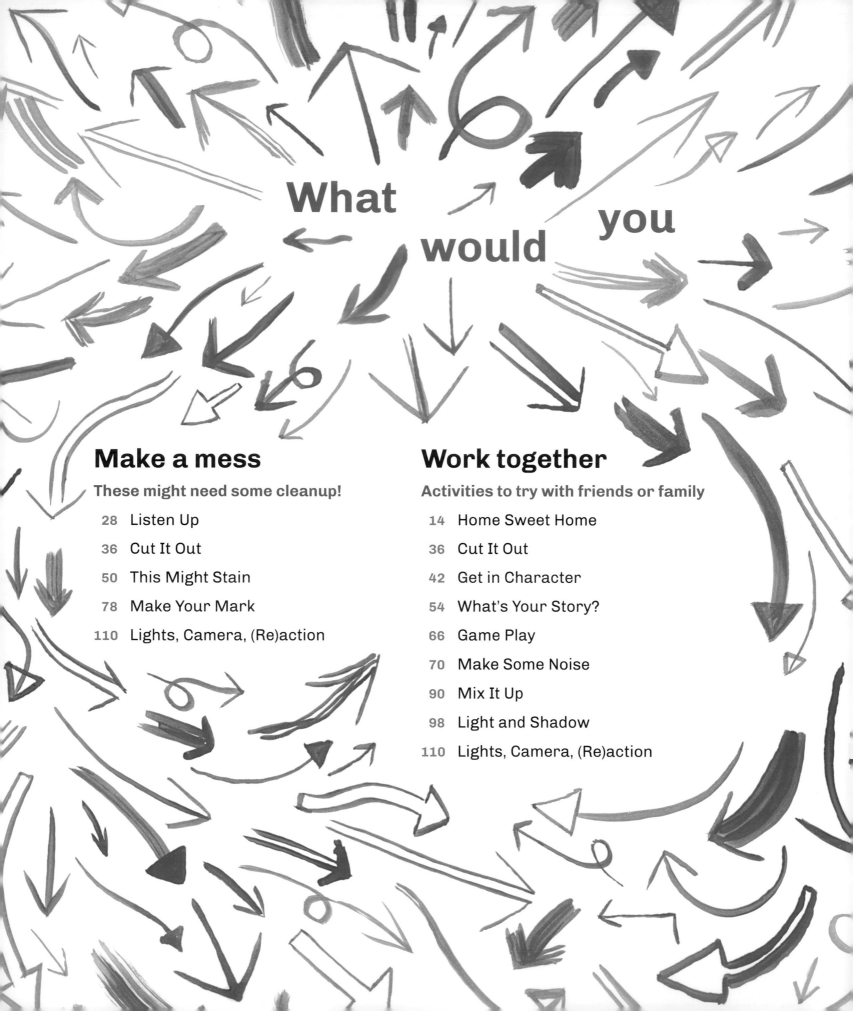

What would you

Make a mess

These might need some cleanup!

Work together

Activities to try with friends or family

like to do?

Scrounge around

Things made with materials you likely have at home

Have some good clean fun

Projects with less mess

About materials

At the start of each activity you'll find a list of all the materials you'll need for that project.

Many of the projects use materials that you might already have at home.

Some activities will ask you to scavenge around your house; you can include materials instead of and in addition to what we suggest.

You might need to buy materials—at an arts and crafts store, office-supply store, or online—for some of the projects.

These lists don't show every material for every project in the book, but they will give you an idea of what kinds of things you'll need.

We suggest ways to use various materials, but the more you play around, the more likely you are to discover new and interesting things to do with them.

Things you'll use over and over again

Colored pencils

Colored paper (construction, fadeless; various sizes)

Copy or printer paper

Crayons or Cray-Pas

Digital camera, camera, or smartphone camera

Glue stick

Scissors

Markers

Pencil

Tape (masking, transparent, duct, washi)

White glue

Stuff to collect

Cardboard boxes (various sizes)

Cardboard rolls (from paper towels, toilet paper, wrapping paper)

Chopsticks

Fabric/fabric scraps

Jar lids

Magazines, catalogs, and newspapers

Packaging materials (bubble wrap, Styrofoam pieces, packing inserts)

Paper bags

Paper and plastic food containers (various shapes and sizes)

Plastic straws

String, yarn, or ribbon

Twist ties

Supplies you may need to purchase

Acetate sheets (various colors)

Adhesive-backed craft foam (any color)

Air-dry clay

Aluminum armature wire (10 or 12 gauge)

Bamboo skewers

Cardstock (various colors)

Clear address labels (1 × 2 ⅝ inches or similar)

Corrugated cardboard roll

Hole punch

Metal fasteners (also called "brads")

Paint (tempera or acrylic)

Paintbrushes (various sizes)

Paper (Bristol, watercolor, patterned, textured, origami; various sizes)

Paper straws

Pipe cleaners (also called "chenille stems")

Plastic-coated craft wire

Removable tape or removable adhesive dots

Washable ink pads (various colors)

Wire cutters

Eames House, Los Angeles, California. 1949

Charles and Ray Eames

Charles and Ray Eames were a husband-and-wife team who designed all kinds of things, from chairs to toys to houses. For their own home they wanted an open space that they could customize (change to fit their needs). They designed a house of glass and steel that lets in light and nature. It has two separate structures: one where they lived and entertained and another where they worked and kept their studio.

Construct a model house.

1 Start by thinking about who will live in your house, what they might do there, and where it's located.

Is it for one person? Two?

Do you imagine your house in a big city?

Or maybe a large family?

Will people need places to work or to play?

Is it a place to gather with friends or to spend time alone?

Do you imagine your house in a the desert?

2 Now, think about the structure and size of your house.

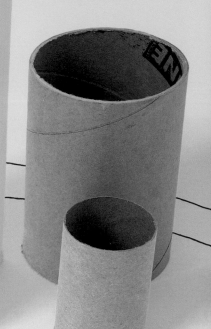

Will your house be round?

Will your house be rectangular?

Will your house have multiple floors?

Will you build out to cover more ground?

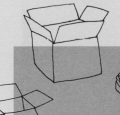

Materials

Tape (masking or washi)

White glue

Scissors

Markers

An assortment of construction materials

Cardboard boxes

Round cardboard containers (such as oatmeal boxes)

Corrugated cardboard roll

Chipboard

Paper or plastic straws

Acetate sheets (various colors)

Construction or fadeless paper (various colors)

Cardboard rolls (from paper towels, toilet paper, wrapping paper)

Packaging materials (bubble wrap, Styrofoam pieces, packing inserts)

Cardstock

Bamboo skewers

Fabric

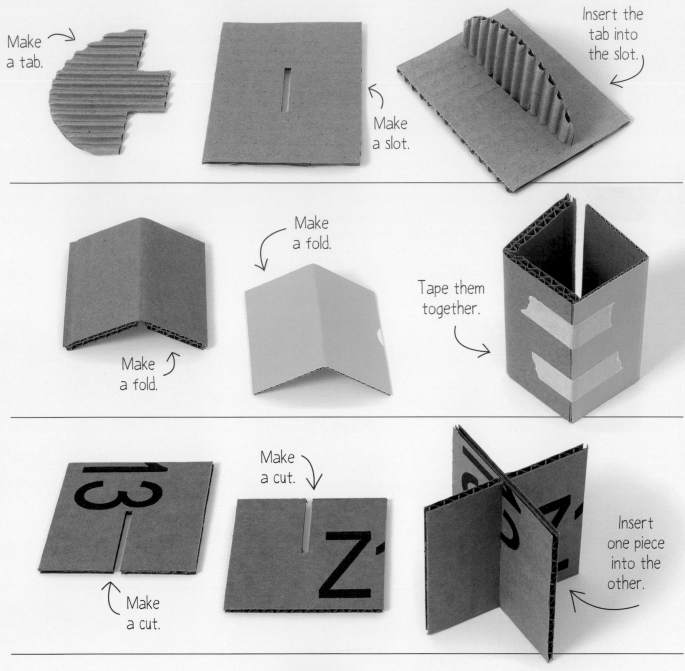

Make a tab.

Make a slot.

Insert the tab into the slot.

Make a fold.

Make a fold.

Tape them together.

Make a cut.

Make a cut.

Insert one piece into the other.

3 Explore construction techniques to figure out which ones work best for the shape of your home.

Make cuts along the bottom.

Spread out and glue.

How can you make your house into a home?

4 Start building! Combine the pieces you've made into a structure.

5 Decorate the surface with different materials or draw on the surface. Add doors, windows, and other details.

ONCE AGAIN, PLEASE

ONCE AGAIN, PLEASE

ONCE AGAIN, PLEASE

ONCE AGAIN, PLEASE

ONCE AGAIN, PLEASE

ONCE AGAIN, PLEASE

ONCE AGAIN, PLEASE

ONCE AGAIN, PLEASE

ONCE AGAIN, PLEASE

Carmela Gross

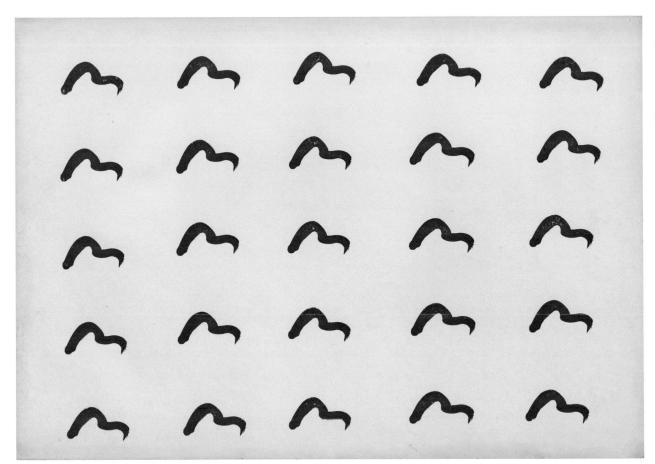

Stamp (Carimbo). 1978

Carmela Gross has created eighty different stamps of squiggles, zig-zags, curved lines, and other marks and gestures. Using one of them at a time, she fills large sheets of paper with single shapes stamped over and over again.

Make your own stamp.

Materials

Washable ink pad (various colors)

Wooden blocks* or the thick lid of a jar

Adhesive-backed craft foam

Paper

Scissors

1 Cut a simple shape or line out of craft foam.

2 Peel the backing from the foam and attach the shape you created to the block.

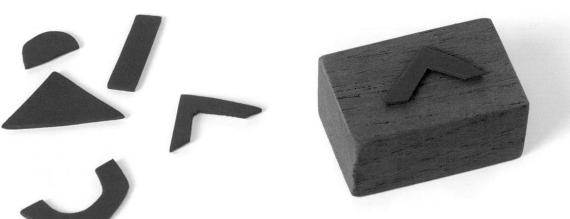

*You can use an old toy block that you don't mind getting ink on.

Press the stamp firmly onto the paper; now press it down lightly.

Make marks close together and then farther apart.

What happens when you rotate your stamp or layer the marks?

3 Start stamping! Try a few different techniques.

4 Create more stamps. You can attach a new shape to a different block, add a shape to another side of the first block, or alter your first stamp by adding new shapes and lines.

Try making different arrangements and patterns with your stamp.

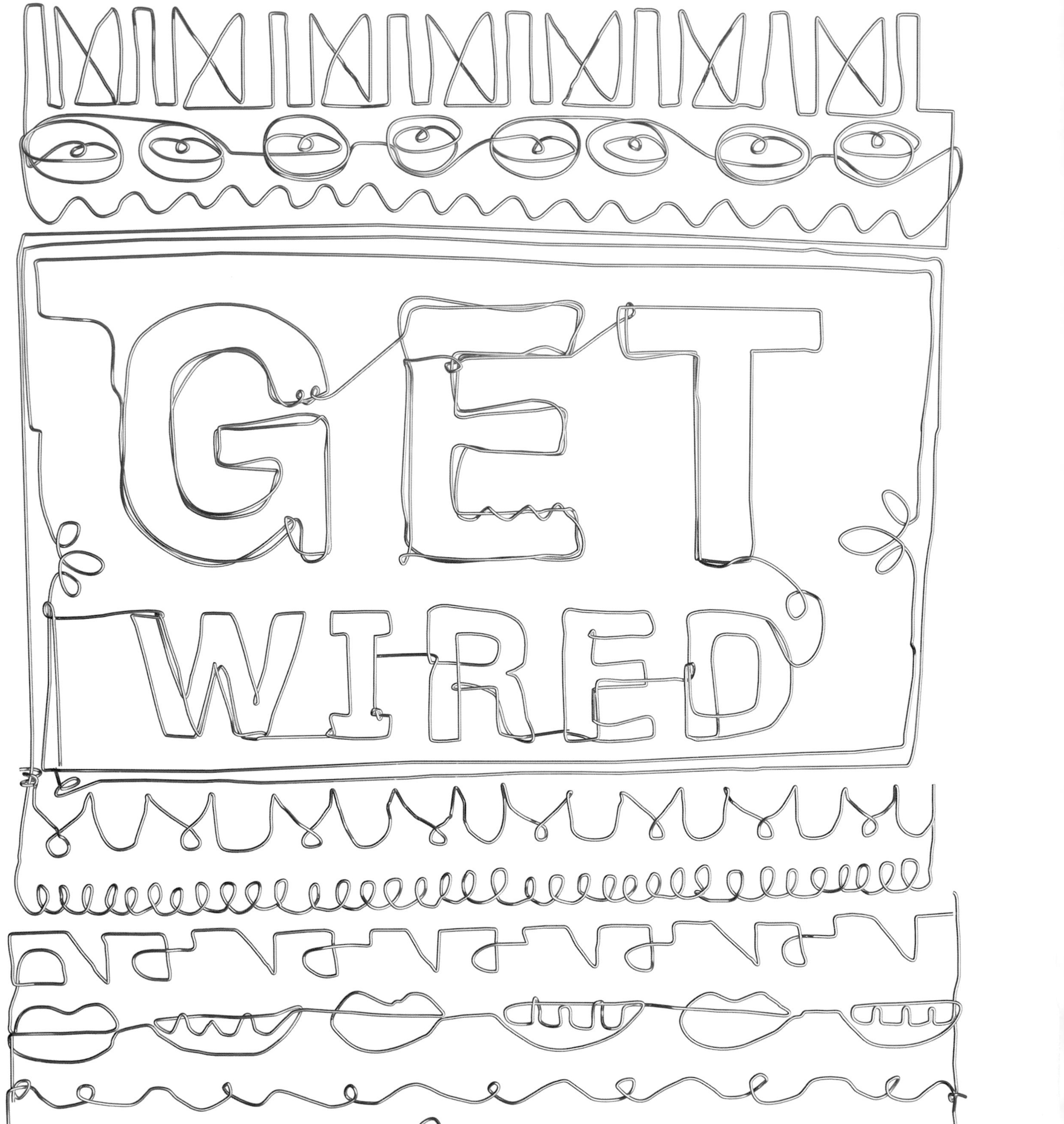
GET
WIRED

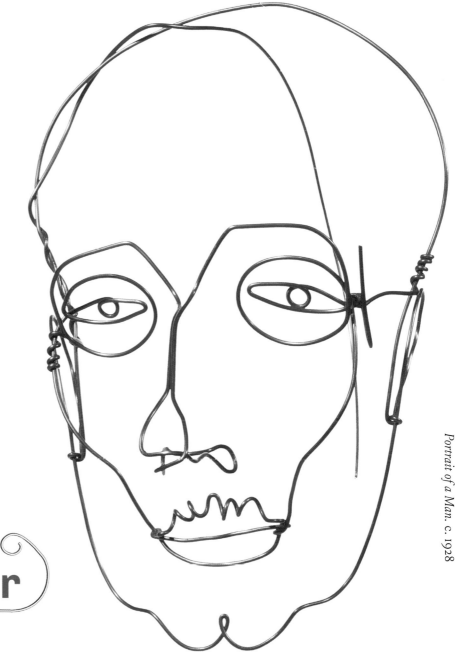

Portrait of a Man. c. 1928

Alexander Calder

Alexander Calder often carried a roll of wire over his shoulder and a pair of pliers in his pocket, and he once commented, "I think best in wire." Calder made different kinds of sculptures out of wire; he made mobiles, moveable sculptures, portraits, and even a miniature circus. He particularly enjoyed working with wire because it allowed him to create "drawings in space."

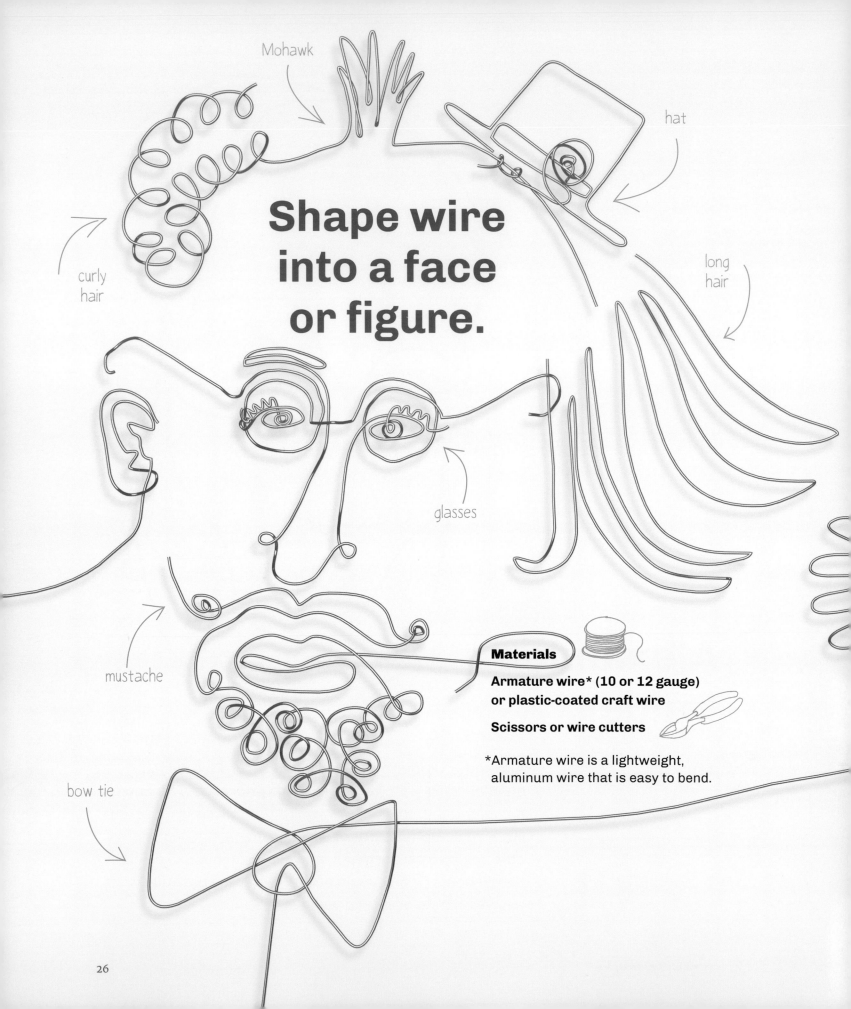

Mohawk

hat

curly
hair

Shape wire into a face or figure.

long
hair

glasses

mustache

Materials

**Armature wire* (10 or 12 gauge)
or plastic-coated craft wire**

Scissors or wire cutters

*Armature wire is a lightweight,
aluminum wire that is easy to bend.

bow tie

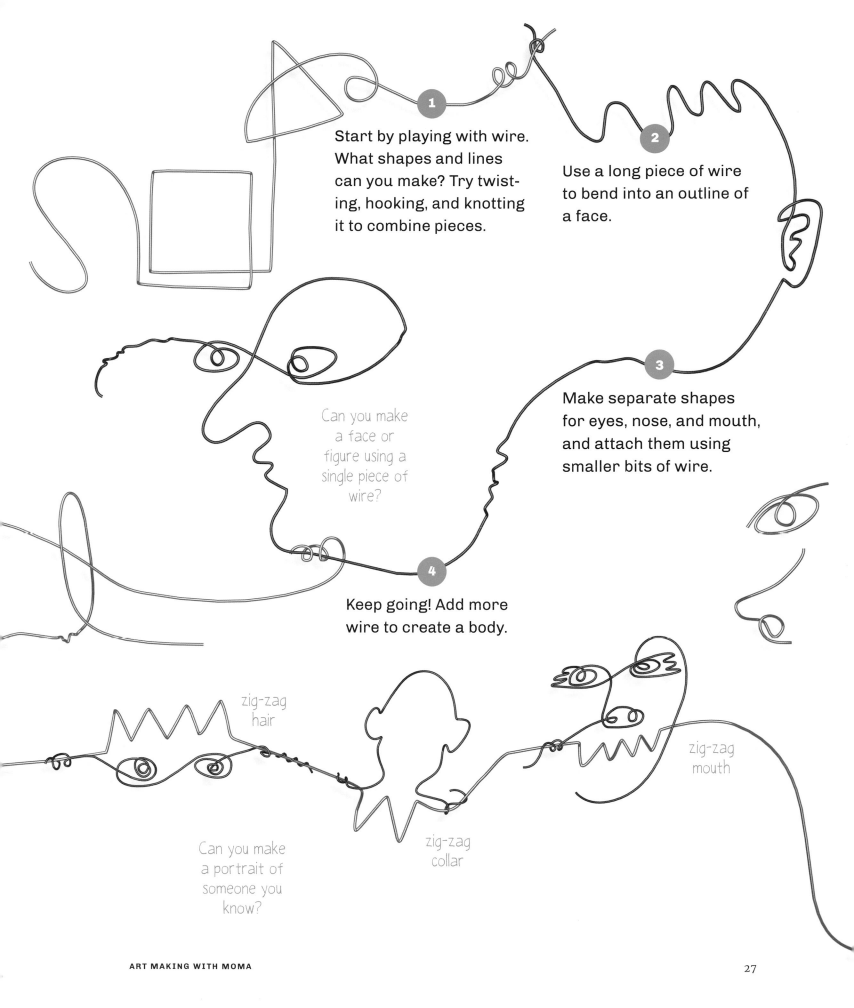

1 Start by playing with wire. What shapes and lines can you make? Try twisting, hooking, and knotting it to combine pieces.

2 Use a long piece of wire to bend into an outline of a face.

3 Make separate shapes for eyes, nose, and mouth, and attach them using smaller bits of wire.

4 Keep going! Add more wire to create a body.

Can you make a face or figure using a single piece of wire?

zig-zag hair

zig-zag collar

zig-zag mouth

Can you make a portrait of someone you know?

Panel for Edwin R. Campbell No. 4. 1914

Vasily Kandinsky

Kandinsky actually saw sounds as colors and lines because of a phenomenon known as synesthesia.

Have you ever felt so moved by music that you wanted to sing, to dance, to paint? Vasily Kandinsky was inspired by music and used colors and lines to capture the different sounds that he heard. After listening to a live performance of music by Arnold Schoenberg—a composer who threw away traditional ideas about harmony and melody—Kandinsky began to change the way he made art. Instead of depicting people and places, he made lines, shapes, and colors themselves the subject of his paintings, a way of working that is known as abstraction.

Paint or draw to music.

1 If you are painting, prepare your workspace by covering a table with newspaper and filling a container of water for cleaning your brushes.

2 Listen to the music.

Is it loud or quiet? Fast or slow?

Can you tap out a steady beat or does the rhythm seem to change?

Tip: Try to use music without words.

Try this alongside a friend. When you've finished, compare your paintings or drawings. Did you use similar colors and lines for the same sounds? Or did you interpret the music differently?

Materials

Paper (Bristol or watercolor)

Paint (tempera or acrylic)

Paintbrushes (small and medium)

Container for cleaning paintbrushes

Newspaper

Music (various styles)

Optional: **Cray-Pas or crayons***

*Painting and drawing materials work equally well for this activity.

3

Now choose a single color to paint or draw with and make marks to show how the music sounds to you.

What kind of line would you use to express a loud instrument?

How might you paint or draw a fast rhythm or strong beat?

4

Try again with different music. Using several colors, show the different sounds that you hear.

Does this look fast or slow?

Romare Bearden

Romare Bearden grew up in Harlem, a neighborhood in New York City. His art celebrates the people who lived there and the sights and sounds he encountered every day. In *The Dove*, a collage, he layered cut-out images of people, objects, and textures that reminded him of his neighborhood.

The Dove. 1964

Create a collage of your neighborhood.

Cut huge shapes and tiny shapes.

Can you use the leftover scraps in your collage?

Materials

Magazines, catalogs, or images printed from the internet

Cardstock or cardboard

White glue or glue stick

Scissors

Optional

Colored pencils

Construction or fadeless paper (various colors)

Paper (patterned and textured)

Brush for glue (small or medium)

1 Think about how would you describe your neighborhood.

Is it filled with tall buildings, or wide-open spaces?

What and who do you see when you walk down the street?

What sounds do you hear?

Tip: You can add colored or patterned paper or your own drawings to your collage.

2 Look through magazines or catalogs or the internet for images that suggest the sights, sounds, and textures of your neighborhood and cut them out.

3 Try different ways of combining your images on paper or cardboard until you have an arrangement you like, and then glue down the pieces.

Tip: If you are using white glue, paint a thin layer all over your paper or cardboard, coating it evenly.

4 Share your collage with friends or family.

What do they notice about your neighborhood in your collage?

Overlap and layer the pieces.

CUT
IT
OUT

Henri Matisse

The Parakeet and the Mermaid. 1952

Henri Matisse used painted paper and scissors to make what he called "cut-outs." His assistants covered white paper with brightly colored paint, and he then "cut directly into color," as he said, to make shapes that reminded him of places: a swimming pool, the sea, a garden. The shapes were pinned to the walls of his dining room and studio, bringing the outdoors inside.

Fill a wall with cut-out shapes.

1 Decide if you will use colored paper or paint paper yourself. If you want to paint paper, fill each page with a solid coat of paint and wait until it dries before cutting.

Tip: When the painted paper dries, it will curl up at the edges. Flatten it under something heavy, such as a stack of books.

Materials

Paper (Bristol)

Paint (tempera or acrylic; various colors)

Paintbrush (medium or large)

Scissors

Removable tape or adhesive dots

Container for cleaning paintbrushes

Optional

Construction or fadeless paper (various colors)

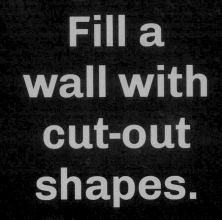

Cut a shape with
only straight lines.

2 Cut various kinds of lines and
shapes with your scissors to
warm up.

Cut a curvy line
from one end of the
paper to the other.

Tip: If you're having
trouble cutting, use a
smaller piece of paper.

Tip: Try turning the paper
as you cut, or holding the
paper steady and moving
the scissors.

The scraps left
behind can be used,
too. These are called
"negative shapes."

3 Imagine a place, such as a beach, garden, park, or forest. Think about what kinds of things you would find there and cut them out of paper in different colors. Don't worry about making them look exactly like the real thing; try to make a basic shape or simplified outline.

Think big! Cut out one or two shapes from each piece of paper.

Overlap shapes.

Fill the wall with shapes so that you feel surrounded by them.

Include both original shapes and their negative shapes.

Turn shapes.

4 Attach removable tape or adhesive dots to the backs of your shapes and fill a wall, window, or refrigerator door with them. Try a few different arrangements.

5 Look at your mural.

In what ways does it remind you of the place you imagined?

In what ways have you created someplace new?

Cindy Sherman

Cindy Sherman creates photographs of herself dressed as different characters, transforming herself through her costume and body language. In every artwork she is both in front of and behind the camera, acting as model, make-up artist, stylist, and photographer. Sherman's portraits suggest a story and invite you to imagine the rest.

"I wish I could treat every day as Halloween, and get dressed up and go out into the world as some eccentric character."
Cindy Sherman

Dress the part, strike a pose, and take a picture.

Materials

Camera or smartphone

Clothes

Props

Optional

Make-up or face paint

Selfie stick or someone to take your photograph

1 Think about a character from a story, movie, TV show, history . . . or perhaps a person you know.

What kinds of clothes and props might transform you into that person?

2 Look around at home and see what you can put together: you might want to invent a character from scratch, based on what you find.

3 Dress up and then try out different poses in a mirror, as if you were in front of a camera.

What can you show by changing your expression and body language?

Is your character serious, playful, or surprised?

Would your character pose for a portrait or be captured in the middle of doing something?

4 Choose a setting or location where you can imagine your character in action—inside, outside, or against a back-drop that you create.

Tip: If you don't have a selfie stick or someone to take your picture, set the timer on your camera.

5 When you are ready, take a photograph of yourself. Capture a few poses and expressions, and then look at your photographs.

What do they show about your character and the story you imagined?

THIS
MIGHT
STAIN

Apple Juice (Tree Top Pure). 1969

Topsoil. 1969

India Ink (Pelikan). 1969

Rose Petal (American Beauty). 1969

Ketchup (Heinz). 1969

Egg Yolk. 1969

Edward Ruscha

Most people try to avoid stains, but Edward Ruscha *made* them! He assembled a list of materials that he thought would leave interesting stains—soil, egg yolk, salad dressing, milk, apple juice, and red cabbage, among others— and used them to stain seventy-six pieces of paper. Ruscha enjoyed the possibilities that come from making art with "overlooked things."

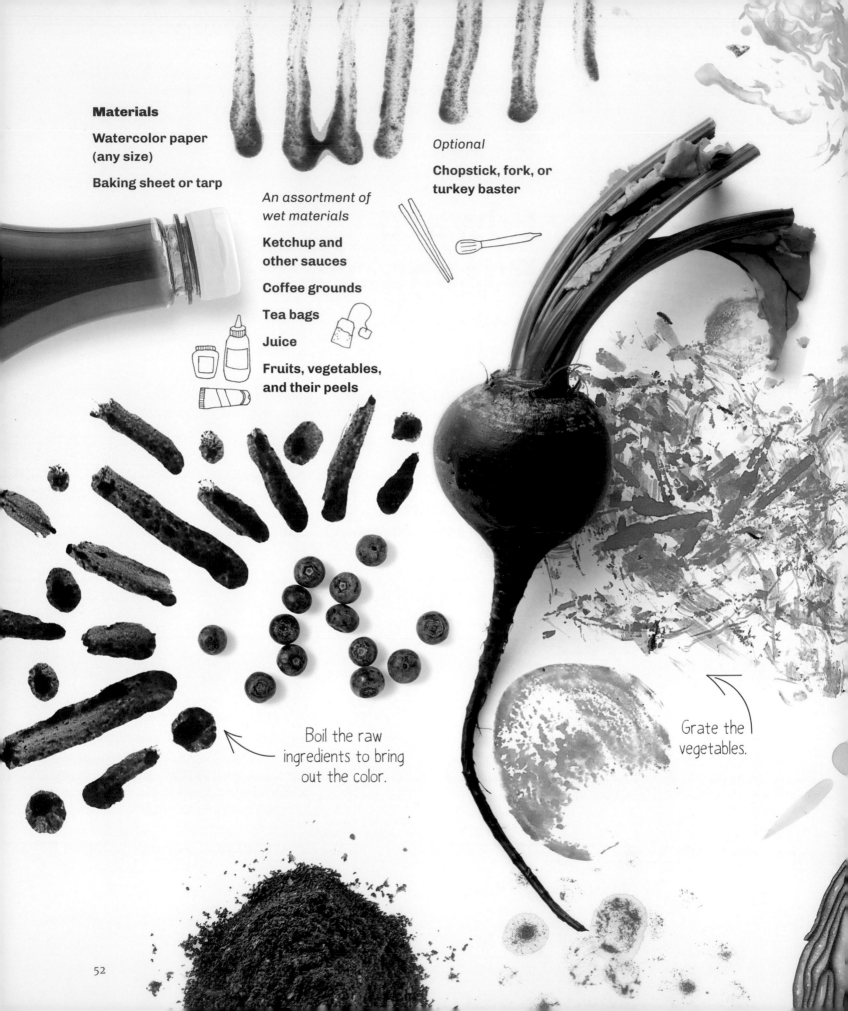

Materials

Watercolor paper (any size)

Baking sheet or tarp

An assortment of wet materials

Ketchup and other sauces

Coffee grounds

Tea bags

Juice

Fruits, vegetables, and their peels

Optional

Chopstick, fork, or turkey baster

Boil the raw ingredients to bring out the color.

Grate the vegetables.

Try pickled vegetables.

Make marks with materials from around your house.

1 Place your paper on top of a baking sheet or a tarp so that you don't stain the table or floor.

2 Apply the materials to the paper in as many different ways as you can think of: pour, drip, squirt, or smear them directly from their containers, or use a tool. You can use your hands to sprinkle or press a material onto the paper, too.

Do any of the stains seem similar to each other?

Do the colors change as they dry?

Tip: You might need only a few drops of some materials. Go slowly until you know what each one is going to do.

3 Give each stain a title. You might use the name of the material or come up with something different.

Tip: Let the stains dry before lifting the paper, so that they don't run or drip down the sheets—unless that's what you want!

WHAT'S YOUR STORY?

what's your story?

Jacob Lawrence

There are many ways to tell a story—through words, through theater and dance, and through visual art. Jacob Lawrence shared the history of an important event by combining words and art in a series of paintings. He told the story of the Great Migration, a period of mass migration in the early twentieth century when many African Americans moved from the American South to cities in the North in search of a better life. Instead of showing every detail, Lawrence selected moments that would show or tell the story in a forceful way, and he illustrated them in sixty different panels. To tie these moments together he repeated shapes and patterns from one panel to the next and used only a few bold colors. He wrote a caption for each painting to add powerful words to his powerful images.

They were very poor. 1940–41

In the North the African American had more educational opportunities. 1940–41

Share a story through pictures.

What's your story? It could be about moving from one place to another or about a trip, a special family event, or an important celebration.

1 Think about your story in three parts—beginning, middle, and end. You will illustrate these main moments in your story on three different panels.

2 For each panel decide who you will include and what they will be doing. Think about how you will show where they are.

3 Make a few quick drawings of your ideas on paper.

4 Using your sketches as a guide, paint the setting of your story and the people in it.

5 When you have finished your paintings, write a short caption for each panel.

Materials

Paper for sketching

Pieces of Bristol board, cardstock, or cardboard (9 × 12 inches, cut in half)

Pencil

Eraser

Paint (tempera or acrylic)

Paintbrushes (small and medium)

Container for cleaning paintbrushes

Fine-tip marker or pen

Need an idea? Talk to an adult about what stories are important to different members of your family.

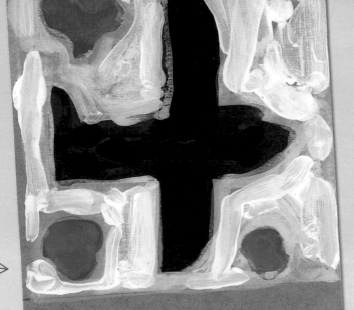

beginning

We flew in a plane to visit my grandfather.

Tip: You can work on one panel at a time or lay them all out and work on them together.

a sample color palette

Tip: Use the same colors, shapes, and textures in each panel to make them look like they are part of the same story.

Grandpa pointed to the mountain and said we will go up there.

middle

At the very top I saw the whole town and even small planes.

end

Furniture Design

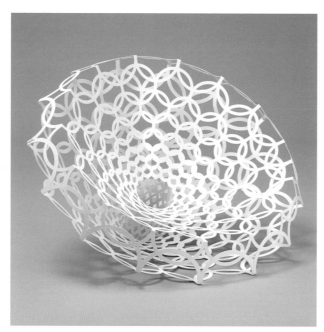

Have you ever thought about what makes a chair . . . a chair? Think about the different kinds of chairs you've sat in and chairs you've seen—comfy padded chairs, stools, rolling chairs, chairs that recline, chairs that fold up, chairs that can be stacked . . . which parts does a chair really need and which parts make it special?

Designers such as Louise Campbell, Fernando Campana, Humberto Campana, and Oki Sato think carefully about function (how the chair should work) and form (how it might look) and what kinds of materials would best achieve these ideas.

Design a chair.

1

Use these questions to figure out what kind of chair you want to make and for whom.

What will be the chair's function—what will it be used for?

☐ Watching TV
☐ Relaxing
☐ Eating
☐ Sitting outdoors, in the park or in a yard
☐ Lounging at a pool
☐ Working at a computer
☐ Reading

What will the chair look like? What parts will you include?

☐ Back
☐ Seat
☐ Arms
☐ Legs (how many?)
☐ Wheels
☐ Cushions

What features will the chair have?

What will it be able to do?

☐ Rock
☐ Swivel
☐ Fold
☐ Swing
☐ Stack
☐ Recline

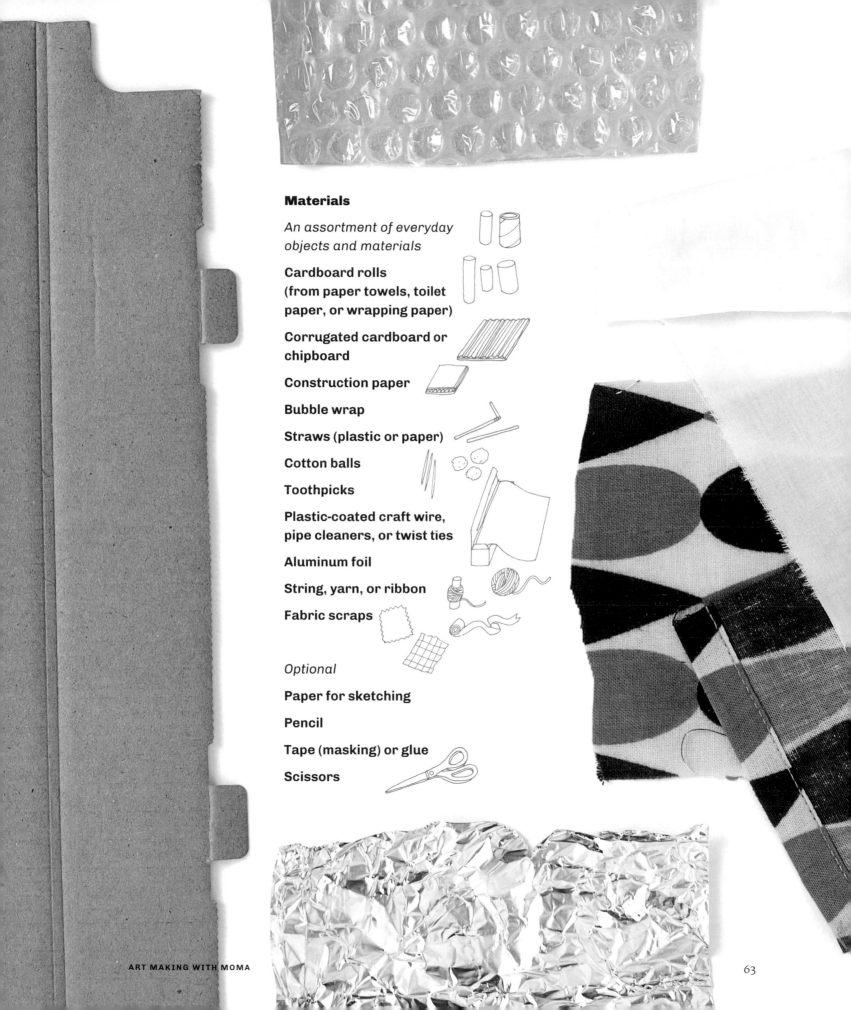

Materials

An assortment of everyday objects and materials

Cardboard rolls (from paper towels, toilet paper, or wrapping paper)

Corrugated cardboard or chipboard

Construction paper

Bubble wrap

Straws (plastic or paper)

Cotton balls

Toothpicks

Plastic-coated craft wire, pipe cleaners, or twist ties

Aluminum foil

String, yarn, or ribbon

Fabric scraps

Optional

Paper for sketching

Pencil

Tape (masking) or glue

Scissors

Sketch a design for your chair or just start experimenting with materials to see what they can do.

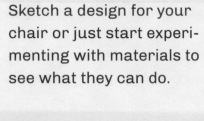

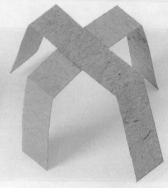

Can you bend, fold, or twist them?

Can they be made to stand on their own?

How might you attach them to other materials?

What qualities do the materials have? Are they soft? Stretchy? Strong?

Do the materials give you ideas about how to use them in a design?

How did the materials you found affect the final design?

Did your design change as you constructed it?

3

Make a model of your chair.

The Surrealists

Max Ernst, André Masson, and Max Morise. *Exquisite Corpse.* 1927

Unreal, dreamlike, bizarre—these words describe the art movement known as Surrealism. The Surrealist artists loved dreams and fantasies; in creative games such as Exquisite Corpse they made artwork out of combinations that were unexpected or unplanned. To play, the artists took turns adding to a drawing without knowing what any of the others had drawn. At the end, the finished drawing was revealed and was always surprising!

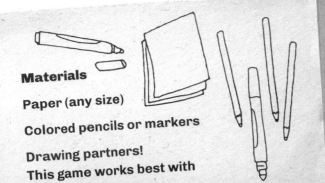

Tip: Add connecting lines into the next section so the next player knows where to begin drawing.

Grab some friends for a Surrealist drawing game.

the head and neck

2 The first person draws a head and neck on the paper's top section.

The player then folds the paper so that the drawn section is hidden.

1 Fold a piece of paper crosswise into as many sections as you have players and then decide who will draw first.

Mix it up! You can draw parts of animals, creatures, or even objects in place of the head, body, or legs.

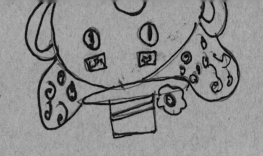

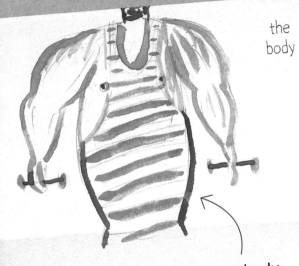

the body

Art by Alexia Doroshenko, Karina Zakabluk, Jason Mats, Bella Sibony

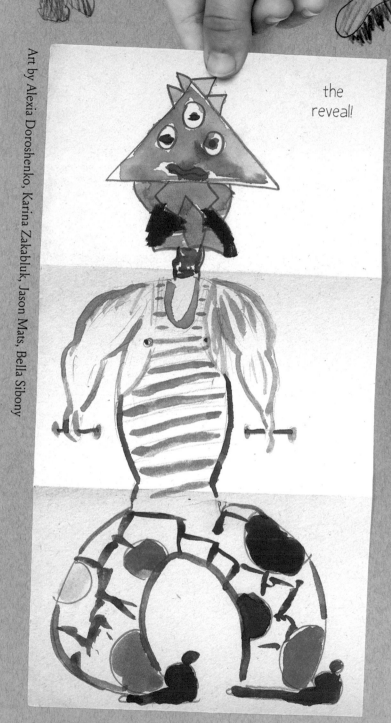

the reveal!

3 The second person draws a body.

4 The third person draws legs and feet. If there are four players, the third player draws just the legs and leaves the feet for the last person.

the legs

5 Once you've all finished, unfold the paper to reveal your Exquisite Corpse.

Soundsuit, 2011

Nick Cave

Nick Cave's Soundsuits are wearable sculptures made from everyday objects and from natural and recycled materials that include twigs, feathers, buttons, beads, and even human hair. The sculptures make sounds as the person wearing it moves, and they can be worn as costumes in performances or shown on their own in exhibitions. Cave travels and collaborates with dancers and musicians in different communities, working with them to create public performances.

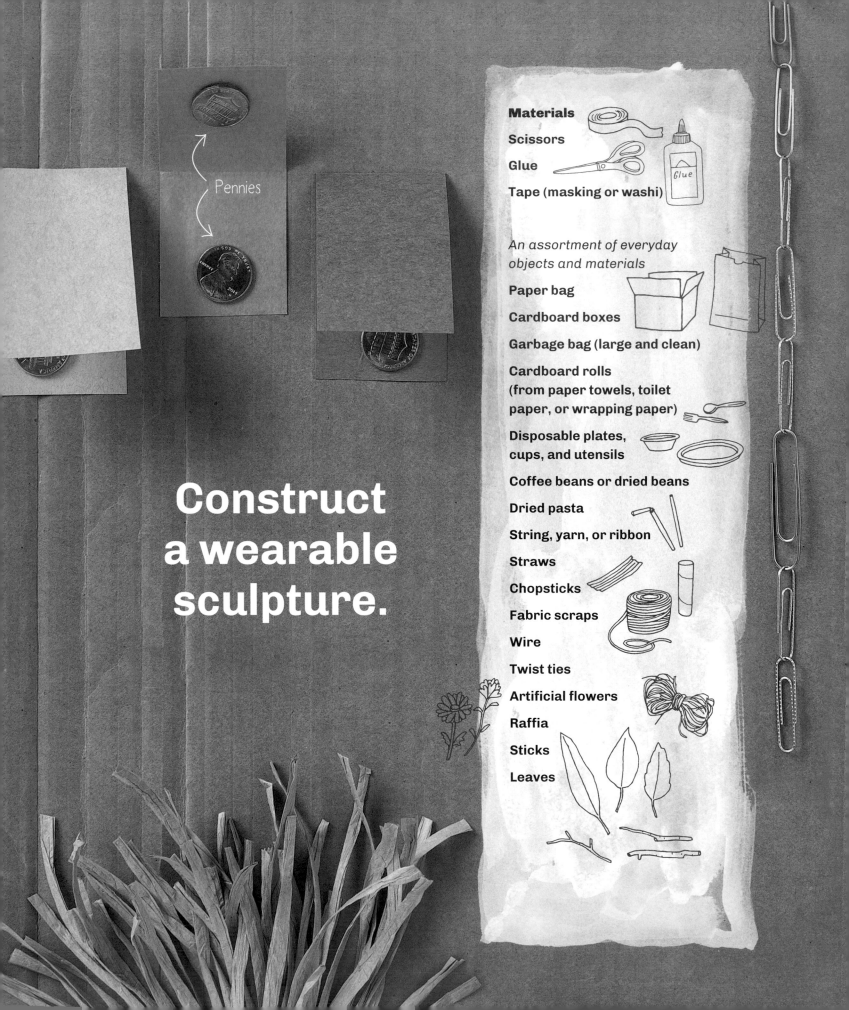

Construct a wearable sculpture.

Pennies

Materials

Scissors

Glue

Tape (masking or washi)

An assortment of everyday objects and materials

Paper bag

Cardboard boxes

Garbage bag (large and clean)

Cardboard rolls (from paper towels, toilet paper, or wrapping paper)

Disposable plates, cups, and utensils

Coffee beans or dried beans

Dried pasta

String, yarn, or ribbon

Straws

Chopsticks

Fabric scraps

Wire

Twist ties

Artificial flowers

Raffia

Sticks

Leaves

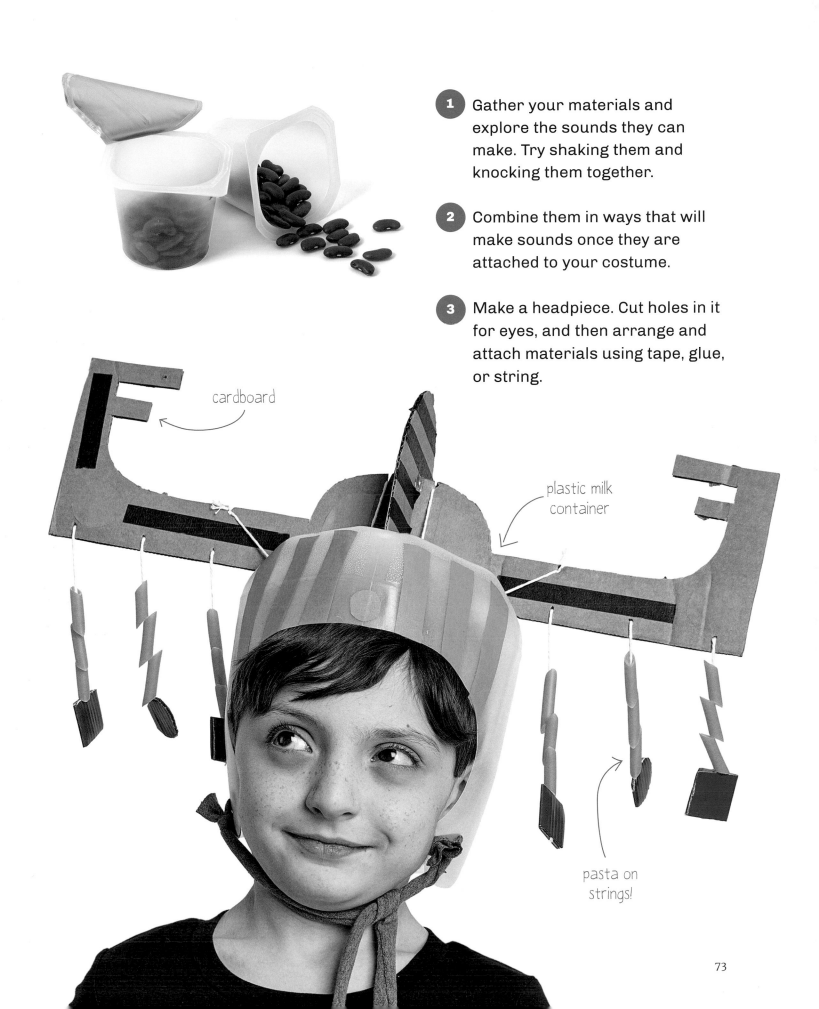

1 Gather your materials and explore the sounds they can make. Try shaking them and knocking them together.

2 Combine them in ways that will make sounds once they are attached to your costume.

3 Make a headpiece. Cut holes in it for eyes, and then arrange and attach materials using tape, glue, or string.

cardboard

plastic milk container

pasta on strings!

RATTLE
RATTLE

Swish
swash
whish

74

SHAKE
SHAKE
SHAKE

4 For the body of your costume, cut arm and neck holes into a large box or garbage bag. This should be done with adult supervision.

5 Add objects and materials to the body of your costume. Try it on with the headpiece every so often as you work, to test how it sounds and feels.

dried beans in plastic cups

balloons taped to garbage bags

6 Put on your finished costume.

How can you move your body to make different sounds? Try moving with music and without.

7 Choreograph or plan a performance and invite a friend to watch.

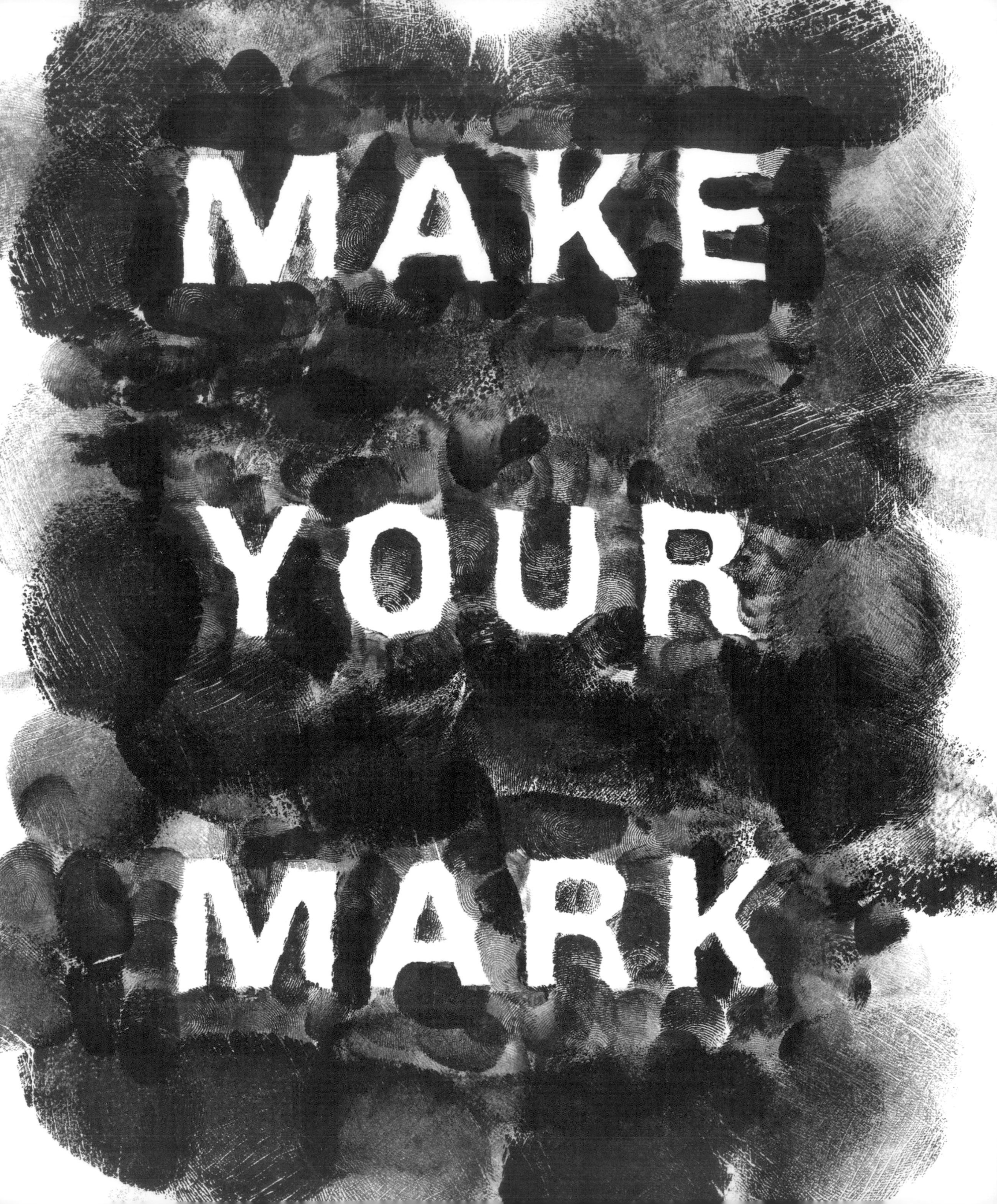
MAKE
YOUR
MARK

Janine Antoni

Have you ever used your body to make art? Janine Antoni has come up with some very imaginative ways to do it. For *Butterfly Kisses* she applied mascara to her eyelashes and quickly blinked, so that her lashes brushed the paper and left fluttery marks. She made 1,254 marks with each eye—a task that took her more than a month.

Butterfly Kisses. 1996–99

Stamp with your body.

Stamp until the ink fades.

Overlap your stamps.

Make a pattern.

Stamp with your toes.

Art by Eve Cohen

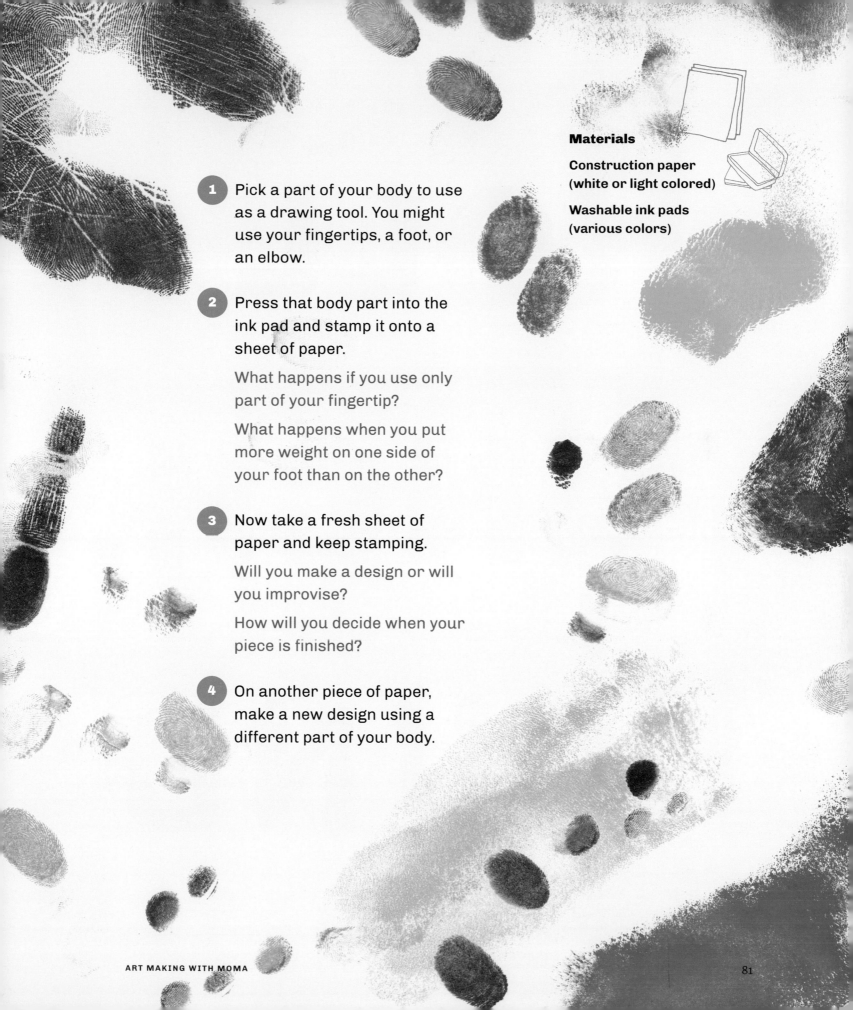

1. Pick a part of your body to use as a drawing tool. You might use your fingertips, a foot, or an elbow.

2. Press that body part into the ink pad and stamp it onto a sheet of paper.

   What happens if you use only part of your fingertip?

   What happens when you put more weight on one side of your foot than on the other?

3. Now take a fresh sheet of paper and keep stamping.

   Will you make a design or will you improvise?

   How will you decide when your piece is finished?

4. On another piece of paper, make a new design using a different part of your body.

Materials

Construction paper
(white or light colored)

Washable ink pads
(various colors)

ROLL, PINCH, POUND

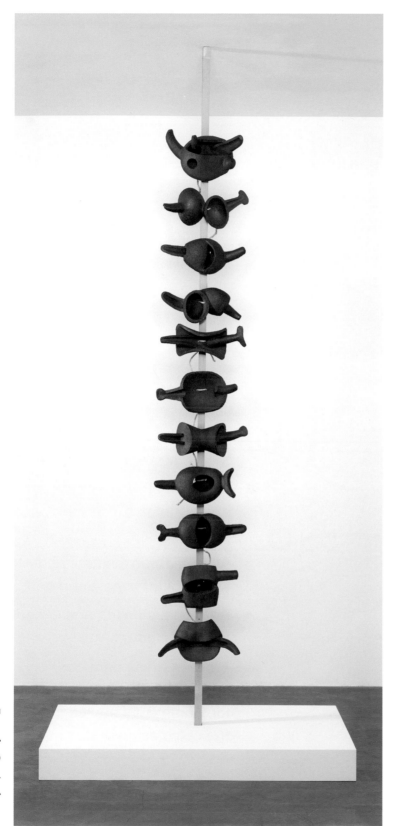

Even the Centipede. 1952

Isamu Noguchi

The shapes in Isamu Noguchi's sculptures and furniture were inspired by his deep connection with nature and his respect for all living things—even the centipedes he found crawling around his house. *Even the Centipede* is a sculpture made of eleven separate red stoneware shapes attached to a wooden pole. At more than thirteen feet tall, it is a towering monument to a very small creature.

Sculpt an animal or insect.

Optional

Fork

Butter knife, wooden craft stick, or dowel

Play dough recipe

Adult supervision recommended

Ingredients

2 cups of flour

1 cup of salt

2 teaspoons of cream of tartar

2 cups of water

4 teaspoons of vegetable oil

Food coloring

1 Combine flour, salt, cream of tartar, and water in a bowl.

2 Pour the oil into a saucepan and put it on the stove over low heat.

3 Add the flour mixture and stir until it forms a stiff ball.

4 Add food coloring and knead it into the dough.

5 Store in an airtight container. It will keep for a long time if it's stored in the refrigerator.

Tip: Wear gloves so the food coloring doesn't stain your hands.

Pinch.

Coil.

Flatten.

Roll.

Stamp with a fork.

Press with your fingers.

Stamp with a dowel.

Combine multiple pieces of clay.

Use just one piece.

1 Play with the clay or play dough to see what kinds of shapes and forms you can make.

2 Add some texture by pressing your fingers, a fork, or a wooden stick into the clay or play dough.

3 Think of an animal or insect that you would like to make. It doesn't have to be an animal you love—it can even be one that frightens you!

4 Form the shapes that make up your creature's body.

Will you make your sculpture one piece or separate pieces?

What details do you need to include to clearly show your animal or insect?

What can you leave out and still express what the animal or insect is like?

Berenice Abbott

The energy, life, and scale of New York City inspired the photographer Berenice Abbott. Many of her black-and-white photographs focused on the shapes, designs, and textures of the city's architecture—its cobblestone streets, elevated trains, storefronts, and tall buildings. She took photographs from different perspectives, looking down on the glowing lights at night from rooftops, up at the city's towers from the street, and through the soaring arches of a train station.

Canyon: Broadway and Exchange Place, Manhattan. 1936
Charles Lane between West and Washington Streets, Manhattan. 1938

Materials

Camera or smartphone

Cardstock or thin
cardboad (4 × 6 inches)

Scissors

Photograph
a place from
different points
of view.

What did you notice that you hadn't before?

88

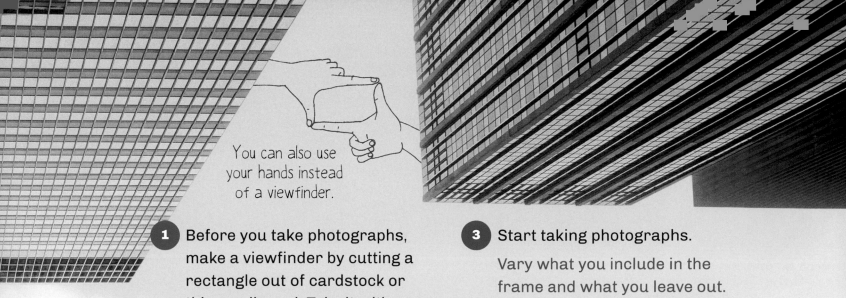

You can also use your hands instead of a viewfinder.

1 Before you take photographs, make a viewfinder by cutting a rectangle out of cardstock or thin cardboard. Take it with you to scout for a location.

2 Look for a place just outside your house or apartment building, on your street, or in your neighborhood.

Using your viewfinder, look for interesting shapes, lines, textures, and shadows.

3 Start taking photographs.

Vary what you include in the frame and what you leave out.

Zoom in on objects to capture details and texture; step back to include more of what's around it.

Try different angles: crouch down low and look up, or climb up and look down.

4 Choose your favorite pictures and share them with your family or friends.

A viewfinder is a tool that frames a small section of what you see in front of you.

The Cubists

In Cubist artworks, people and objects are often shown from several angles at once. The light, shadows, colors, and space in the paintings combine in an image that seems fractured or broken. Diego Rivera used these techniques, which had been pioneered by Pablo Picasso and Georges Braque, to make a portrait of Jacques Lipchitz, his friend and fellow artist. Even though the portrait doesn't look exactly like Lipchitz, we can recognize details of the face and body in it.

front view

left side view

Combine multiple points of view into a single portrait.

right side view

Materials

Clear address labels
(1 × 2 ⅝ inches each, or similar)

White paper (9 × 6 inches)

Pencil

Colored pencils

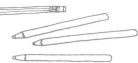

1 Ask a friend or family member to be your model, or draw someone from memory.

2 Make a few practice sketches of your model's face on paper.

3 Cut the clear sheet of labels into four sections. Use three of them to draw your model's face from three different points of view (front, right side, left side), with one point of view on each sheet.

4 Peel off the labels, and then combine them on your paper to create a single mixed-up portrait.

Tip: Draw all the way to the edges of the sheets so your drawings are the same size.

all the
views
combined

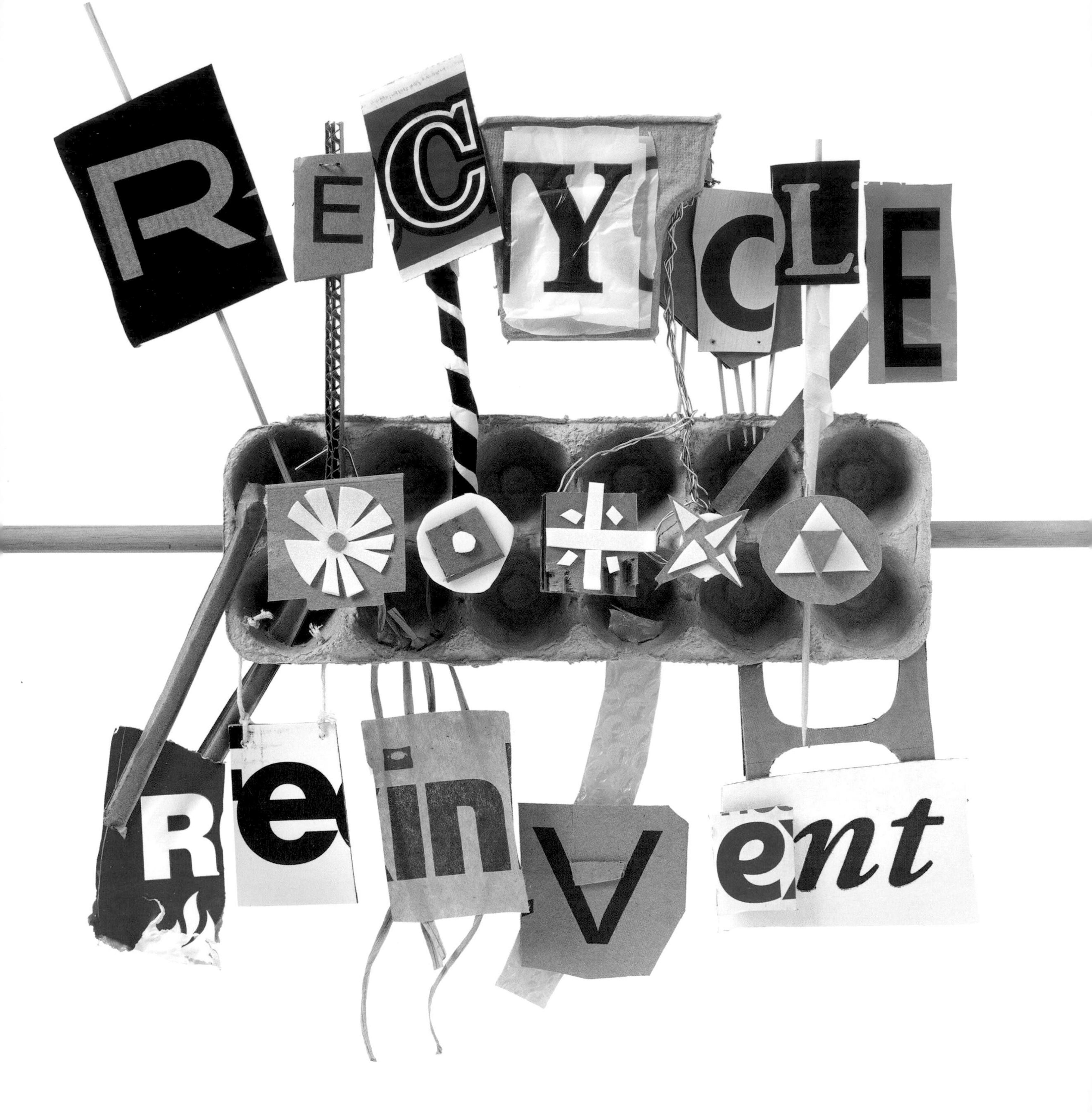
RECYCLE
reinvent

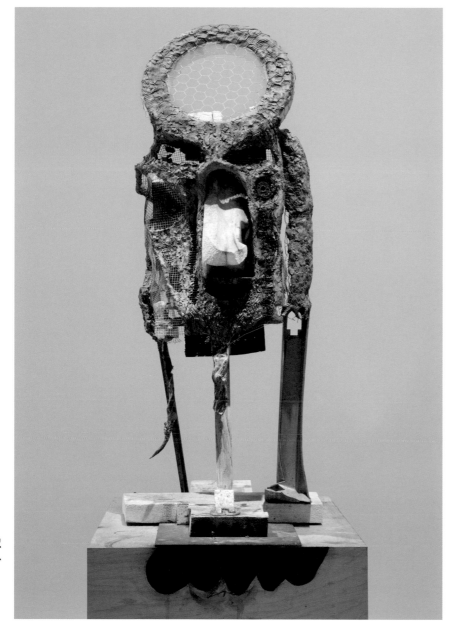

Bleekmen. 2010

Huma Bhabha

Huma Bhabha collects materials that other people have thrown away, such as wire, Styrofoam, and wood, and combines them in sculptures with wax, plaster, and clay. She has said that her works are inspired by crumbling buildings, nature, and science fiction. Many of her sculptures have masklike faces and look like they might have been made a long time ago, or like they come from another world, light-years away.

Tie pieces
together
with string
or wire.

Cut slits
and tabs.

Punch
holes.

Apply tape.

Tip: As you build
your sculpture, look
at it from all sides.

Use clay or
play dough
as a base.

Combine materials to create a sculpture.

1

Try different ways of combining
and arranging the materials
you have gathered.

What do the shapes and textures of the various materials
make you think of?

2

Put it all together! Materials
can be attached to each other
in different ways.

Tip: You don't have to know in advance
what your sculpture is going to be—
whether it will be a person, an animal,
a creature, a machine, or some
combination of all of them!

See page 18 for
construction tips.

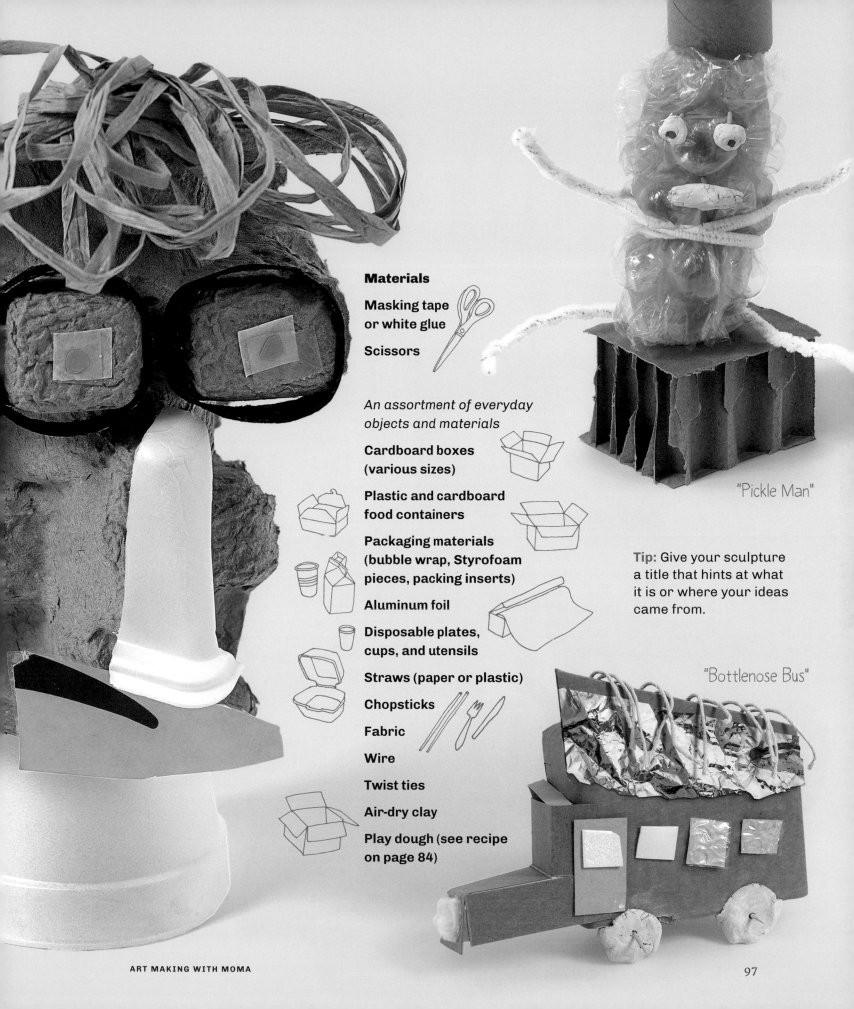

Materials

Masking tape or white glue

Scissors

An assortment of everyday objects and materials

Cardboard boxes (various sizes)

Plastic and cardboard food containers

Packaging materials (bubble wrap, Styrofoam pieces, packing inserts)

Aluminum foil

Disposable plates, cups, and utensils

Straws (paper or plastic)

Chopsticks

Fabric

Wire

Twist ties

Air-dry clay

Play dough (see recipe on page 84)

"Pickle Man"

Tip: Give your sculpture a title that hints at what it is or where your ideas came from.

"Bottlenose Bus"

LIGHT

LIGHT

AND

AND

SHADOW

SHADOW

Lotte Reiniger

Lotte Reiniger's animated films are some of the first in movie history. They are based on fairy tales and operas, and are filled with magic and adventure. Reiniger used silhouette animation, a technique she pioneered in the 1920s, to make her films. She cut intricate puppets and scenery out of paper, and then she posed and photographed the puppets on a surface lit from below. By slowly changing the figures' positions and taking photographs of each adjustment, she created a series of movements that came together to tell a story.

Materials

Cardstock or thick construction paper (black)

Hole punch

Metal fasteners (also called "brads")

Scissors

Optional

White pencil

Put on a show

Cardboard box (medium or large size)

White copy or printer paper

Tape (Scotch and masking)

Dowels or chopsticks

Flashlight

Make a stop-motion film

Cell phone camera

Tripod or camera stand*

Stop-motion animation app

*Make your own camera stand:

Cardboard box (medium or large size)

Flashlight or desk lamp

Make silhouette puppets and put on a show.

Tip: To show facial features (like a nose, mouth, and chin) cut your figure's head in profile (from the side) or fold your paper and cut them out.

1. Pick a story to tell. It can be a version of a story you already know, or an invented one that's entirely new.

   How many characters are there? How many puppets will you need?

2. To make your puppets, cut separate shapes out of black paper for heads, bodies, arms, and legs. The more parts you make, the more your puppet can move and take different poses.

   You can also make a puppet in a single shape with no moving parts.

3. Put your puppet together by punching or poking holes where you want to join pieces. Line up the holes and put metal fasteners through them.

4. Cut out simple props such as trees and chairs for your story's setting.

Line up the holes and attach the brad.

Tip: It may help to draw the shapes of the body parts before you cut them; use white pencil on the black paper.

Option 1
Put on a show

1 With tape, attach a stick to the back of each puppet's body. Add more sticks to its arms and legs if you want those parts to move.

2 Make your theater using a cardboard box and white paper. Cut a rectangular hole out of the side of the box. Cover the hole with paper and tape the paper in place.

Tip: Make sure to pick a box that is big enough to fit the height of your puppets!

Tape the top down.

Cover this hole with a piece of white paper.

Cut a big hole in the back.

Leave some extra space on the bottom for your hands.

Position the flashlight in the back.

3 Shine a flashlight on the inside of your theater, turn off the lights, and put on your show!

Option 2

Make a stop-motion film

1 Download an app for stop-motion animation on a smartphone or tablet. You'll use the application to photograph your puppets from above, and it will stitch them together into a continuous film.

Position your camera/phone so you can take photos.

Position your light so it shines through the hole on top.

This paper will be the backdrop to the animation. You can choose white, or another color.

2 Place your puppet on a flat surface. If you have a tripod, angle your smartphone or tablet downward over your puppet. Skip to step 4.

3 If you don't have a tripod, you can make a stand for your camera using a cardboard box.

Lay a box on its side with the open flaps facing you and cut a medium-size hole in the top.

Tip: Start your hole in the middle and cut a rectangle off to one side, so that you can position the camera lens in the center and capture the whole image below.

Position the camera and shine a light such as a desk lamp into the hole.

Place a light-colored piece of paper inside of the box, on the bottom, with your puppet(s) on it.

Tip: You may have to make a few adjustments to the size of your hole to make sure your puppet is in the frame and evenly lit.

4 Take a picture, move the puppet slightly, and then take another picture. Repeat until you have told your whole story, frame by frame.

5 When you are finished, share your animation with friends!

Tip: It takes about ten photographs to make one second of film, so you might want to add to your project bit by bit.

ALL
ABOUT
ME

Frida Kahlo

Frida Kahlo painted self-portraits and filled them with symbols of her ideas, her feelings, and important events in her life. In *Fulang-Chang and I,* Kahlo painted herself wearing traditional Mexican clothing, surrounded by native plants to show her pride in her country. She also included her pet monkey—connected to her by a pink ribbon—perhaps illustrating her love for him.

When Kahlo gave the painting to her friend Mary Sklar, she added a mirror to be hung next to it, so that when her friend looked in the mirror they would be together—her face and Mary's reflection—even when they were physically apart.

Create a self-portrait.

1 Draw or paint a picture of yourself. It can be a close-up view of your face, or you can include part or all of your body.

2 To get started, look in a mirror and think about the shapes that make up your face. Use these simple shapes to start your portrait, and then fill in the details.

3 Decide what else you will include to suggest who you are and how you see yourself.

Will you draw yourself in the kinds of clothes you wear every day, in a costume, or an imagined outfit?

Will you include a setting that's familiar, or one that's invented?

Art by Sophia Privine, Ida Weills, Eve Cohen, Henry Marks, Maxine Paul-Emile, Genesis Solange Pittman

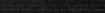

Instead of drawing, you can use a photograph. Cut out the figure from the background and glue it to a piece of paper, and then draw in the setting and add some of your favorite things.

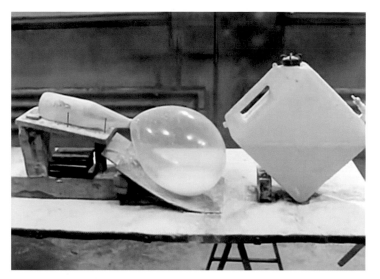

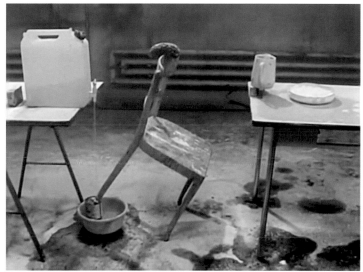

Peter Fischli and David Weiss

Can you imagine an action movie starring objects instead of people? Peter Fischli and David Weiss, artists who often worked together, made art from ordinary and industrial materials used in unexpected ways. To make *The Way Things Go* they gathered objects such as tires, balloons, and old shoes to create a series of chain reactions, including a rolling tire knocking over a board that sends a ladder "walking" down a ramp, and a water bottle shooting foam that oozes down a plank and extinguishes a pair of candles.

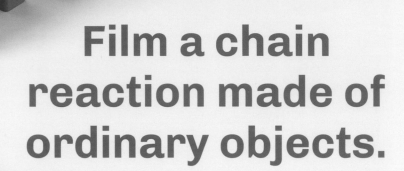

Film a chain reaction made of ordinary objects.

Make a ramp.

1

Gather materials and try various setups to see how each one moves and how it might cause others to move:

Roll a ball, toy car, or metal can down a ramp.

Arrange three or more blocks, books, cereal boxes, or dominos a few inches apart and knock the first one into the next.

Tie one end of a string around a small block, ball, or slightly heavy object (or use a yo-yo). Tie the other end to a doorknob and start the object swinging back and forth. You've made a pendulum!

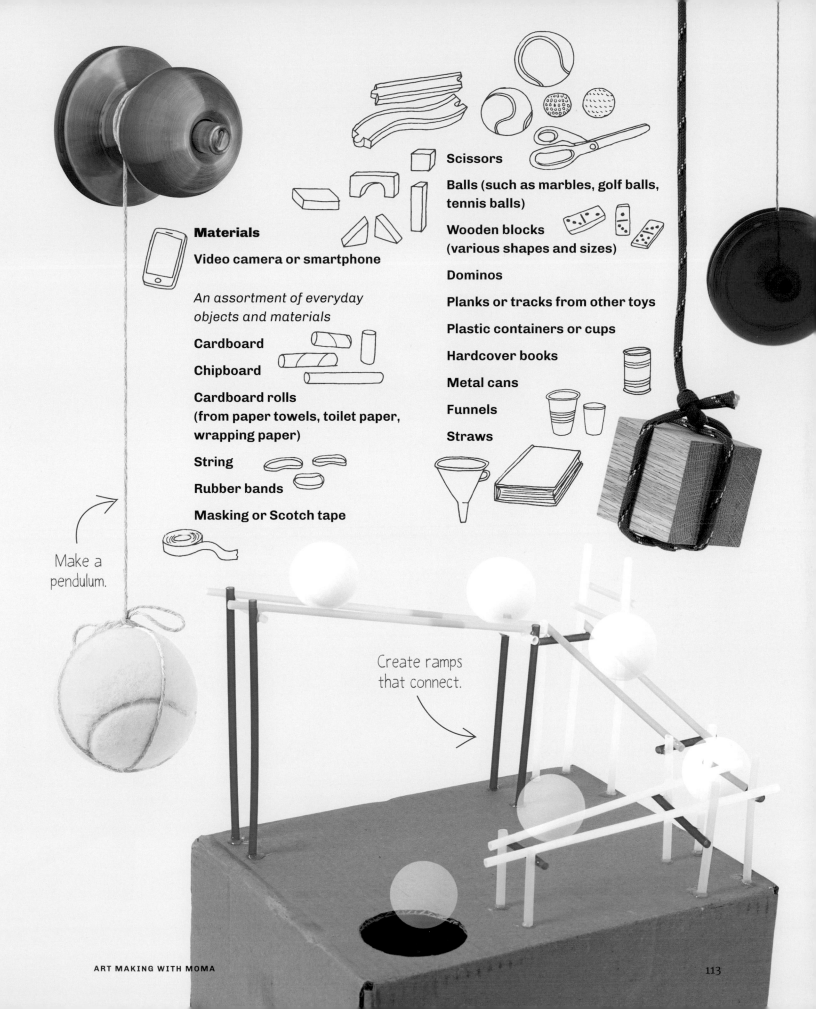

Make a
pendulum.

Materials

Video camera or smartphone

*An assortment of everyday
objects and materials*

Cardboard

Chipboard

Cardboard rolls
**(from paper towels, toilet paper,
wrapping paper)**

String

Rubber bands

Masking or Scotch tape

Scissors

**Balls (such as marbles, golf balls,
tennis balls)**

Wooden blocks
(various shapes and sizes)

Dominos

Planks or tracks from other toys

Plastic containers or cups

Hardcover books

Metal cans

Funnels

Straws

Create ramps
that connect.

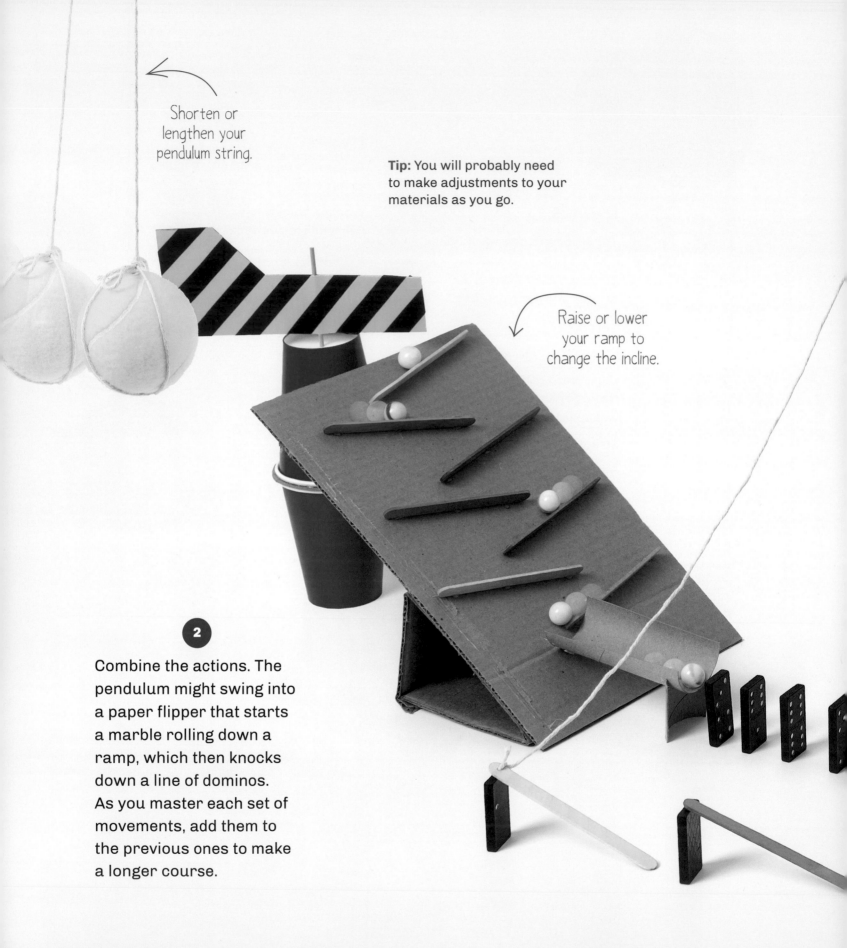

Shorten or lengthen your pendulum string.

Tip: You will probably need to make adjustments to your materials as you go.

Raise or lower your ramp to change the incline.

2

Combine the actions. The pendulum might swing into a paper flipper that starts a marble rolling down a ramp, which then knocks down a line of dominos. As you master each set of movements, add them to the previous ones to make a longer course.

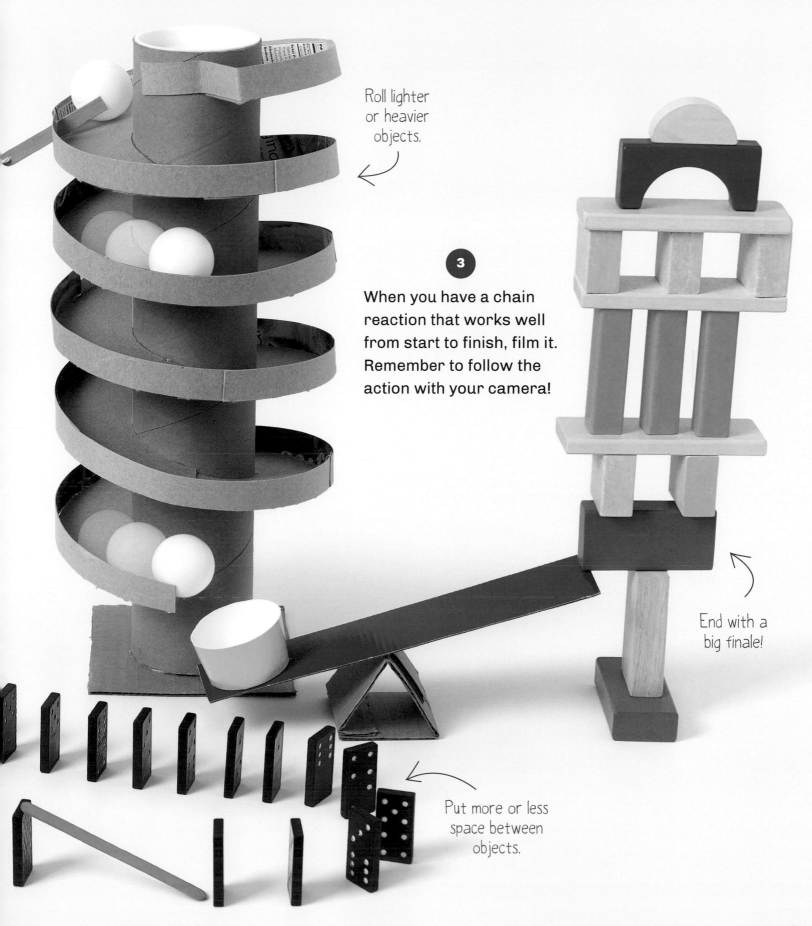

Roll lighter or heavier objects.

3

When you have a chain reaction that works well from start to finish, film it. Remember to follow the action with your camera!

End with a big finale!

Put more or less space between objects.

Berenice Abbott
(American, 1898–1991)
*Canyon: Broadway and Exchange
Place, Manhattan.* 1936
Gelatin silver print, 9¼ × 7¼ in.
(23.5 × 18.4 cm)
The Museum of Modern Art,
New York. Gift of the Board of
Education, the City of New York
87

Berenice Abbott
(American, 1898–1991)
*Charles Lane between West and
Washington Streets, Manhattan.* 1938
Gelatin silver print, 9⁷⁄₁₆ × 6⁷⁄₈ in.
(24 × 17.5 cm)
The Museum of Modern Art,
New York. Gift of the Robert and
Joyce Menschel Foundation
87

Janine Antoni
(American, born 1964)
Butterfly Kisses. 1996–99
Cover Girl Thick Lash mascara
on paper, 29¾ × 30 in.
(75.6 × 76.2 cm)
The Museum of Modern Art,
New York. Purchase
79

Romare Bearden
(American, 1911–1988)
The Dove. 1964
Cut-and-pasted printed paper,
gouache, pencil, and colored
pencil on board, 13⅜ × 18¾ in.
(33.8 × 47.5 cm)
The Museum of Modern Art,
New York. Blanchette Hooker
Rockefeller Fund
33

Huma Bhabha
(American, born Pakistan, 1962)
Bleekmen. 2010
Clay, wood, wire, Styrofoam,
plastic, cast iron, fabric,
aluminum, synthetic polymer
paint, ink, paper, and brass wire,
7 ft. 8½ in. × 36 in. × 31½ in.
(235 × 91.4 × 80 cm)
The Museum of Modern Art,
New York. Gift of the Speyer
Family Foundation
95

Alexander Calder
(American, 1898–1976)
Portrait of a Man. c. 1928
Brass wire, 12⅞ × 8¾ × 13½ in.
(32.5 × 22.2 × 34.2 cm)
The Museum of Modern Art,
New York. Gift of the artist
25

Fernando Campana (Brazilian, born 1961) and Humberto Campana (Brazilian, born 1953)
Vermelha Chair. 1993
Iron with epoxy coating, aluminum, and cord,
31 × 29 ⅛ × 22 ¾ in.
(78.7 × 74 × 57.8 cm)
The Museum of Modern Art, New York. Gift of Patricia Phelps de Cisneros
61

Louise Campbell
(Danish, born 1970)
Veryround Chair. 2006
Laser-cut sheet steel,
27 ³⁄₁₆ × 41 ⁹⁄₁₆ × 32 ¹¹⁄₁₆ in.
(69 × 105.5 × 83 cm)
The Museum of Modern Art, New York. Gift of the manufacturer
61

Nick Cave
(American, born 1959)
Soundsuit. 2011
Found objects, knit head and bodysuit, and mannequin,
10 ft. 1 in. × 42 in. × 33 in. (307.3 × 106.7 × 83.8 cm)
The Museum of Modern Art, New York. Gift of Agnes Gund in honor of Dr. Stuart W. Lewis
71

Charles Eames (American, 1907–1978) and Ray Eames (American, 1912–1988)
Eames House, Los Angeles, California. 1949
Plastic and wood, 20 × 84 × 30 in.
(50.8 × 213.4 × 76.2 cm)
The Museum of Modern Art, New York. Emilio Ambasz Fund
15

Max Ernst (French and American, born Germany, 1891–1976), André Masson (French, 1896–1987), and Max Morise (French, 1900–1973)
Exquisite Corpse. 1927
Color crayons on paper, 8 × 6 in.
(20.8 × 15.5 cm)
Musée national d'art moderne, Centre Georges-Pompidou, Paris
67

Peter Fischli (Swiss, born 1952) and David Weiss (Swiss, 1946–2012)
The Way Things Go. 1987
16mm film transferred to video (color, sound), 31 min
The Museum of Modern Art, New York. Purchase
111

Carmela Gross
(Brazilian, born 1946)
Stamp (Carimbo). 1978
Stamped ink on paper,
composition (irreg.) 24 3/16 ×
33 3/4" in. (61.5 × 85.7 cm); sheet
27 11/16 × 39 5/16 in. (70.3 × 99.8 cm)
The Museum of Modern Art,
New York. Gift of Andrea and
José Olympio da Veiga Pereira
in honor of Luis Enrique Pérez
Oramas
21

Frida Kahlo
(Mexican, 1907–1954)
Fulang-Chang and I. 1937
(assembled after 1939)
Oil on composition board (1937)
with painted mirror frame (added
after 1939), and mirror with
painted mirror frame (after 1939),
framed painting 22 1/4 × 17 3/8 × 1 3/4
in. (56.5 × 44.1 × 4.4 cm);
framed mirror 25 1/4 × 19 × 1 3/4 in.
(64.1 × 48.3 × 4.4 cm)
The Museum of Modern Art,
New York. Mary Sklar Bequest
107

Vassily Kandinsky
(French, born Russia, 1866–
1944)
*Panel for Edwin R. Campbell
No. 4*. 1914
Oil on canvas, 64 1/4 × 48 1/4 in.
(163 × 122.5 cm)
The Museum of Modern Art,
New York. Nelson A. Rockefeller
Fund (by exchange)
29

Jacob Lawrence
(American, 1917–2000)
*The migrants arrived in great
numbers*. 1940–41
Casein tempera on hardboard,
12 × 18 in. (30.5 × 45.7 cm)
The Museum of Modern Art,
New York. Gift of Mrs. David
M. Levy
55

Jacob Lawrence
(American, 1917–2000)
They were very poor. 1940–41
Casein tempera on hardboard,
12 × 18 in. (30.5 × 45.7 cm)
The Museum of Modern Art,
New York. Gift of Mrs. David
M. Levy
56

Jacob Lawrence
(American, 1917–2000)
*In the North the African American
had more educational opportunities*.
1940–41
Casein tempera on hardboard,
18 × 12 in. (45.7 × 30.5 cm)
The Museum of Modern Art,
New York. Gift of Mrs. David
M. Levy
56

Jacob Lawrence
(American, 1917–2000)
The migration gained in momentum.
1940–41
Casein tempera on hardboard,
18 × 12 in. (45.7 × 30.5 cm)
The Museum of Modern Art,
New York. Gift of Mrs. David
M. Levy
57

Henri Matisse
(French, 1869–1954)
The Parakeet and the Mermaid
(*La Perruche et la Sirène*). 1952
Gouache on paper, cut and
pasted, and charcoal on white
paper (11 ft. ⅝ in. × 25 ft. 2½ in.
(337 × 768.5 cm)
Collection Stedelijk Museum,
Amsterdam. Acquired with
the generous support of the
Vereniging Rembrandt and the
Prins Bernhard Cultuurfonds
37

nendo (Japan, established 2002),
Oki Sato (Canadian, born 1977)
Cabbage Chair. 2007
Pleated paper, roll 36 × 20 in.
(91.4 × 50.8 cm); opened
29 × 33 in. (73.7 × 83.8 cm)
The Museum of Modern Art,
New York. Gift of the designer
61

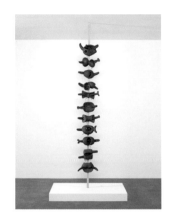

Isamu Noguchi
(American, 1904–1988)
Even the Centipede. 1952
Unglazed Kasama red stoneware,
wood pole, and hemp cord,
13 ft. 9⅝ in. × 18 in.
(420.6 × 46 cm)
The Museum of Modern Art,
New York. A. Conger Goodyear
Fund
83

Lotte Reiniger
(German, 1899–1981)
Die Abenteuer des Prinzen Achmed
(*The Adventures of Prince Achmed*).
1926
35mm film (color, silent), 65 min.
The Museum of Modern
Art, New York. Gift of James
Brewster, Young American Films
99

Diego Rivera
(Mexican, 1886–1957)
Young Man in a Gray Sweater
(*Jacques Lipchitz*). 1914
Oil on canvas, 25⅝ × 21⅝ in.
(65.1 × 54.9 cm)
The Museum of Modern
Art, New York. Gift of
T. Catesby Jones
91

Edward Ruscha
(American, born 1937)
Stains. 1969
Portfolio of seventy-six mixed-
medium stains, composition:
varies; sheet, each: 11⅞ × 10¾ in.
(30.2 × 27.3 cm)
Publisher: Heavy Industry
Publications, Hollywood
Printer: the artist, Los Angeles
Edition: 70
The Museum of Modern Art,
New York. Gift of Iolas Gallery
Top to bottom, left to right:
Apple Juice (Tree Top Pure);
Topsoil; India Ink (Pelikan); Rose
Petal (American Beauty); Ketchup
(Heinz); Egg Yolk.
51

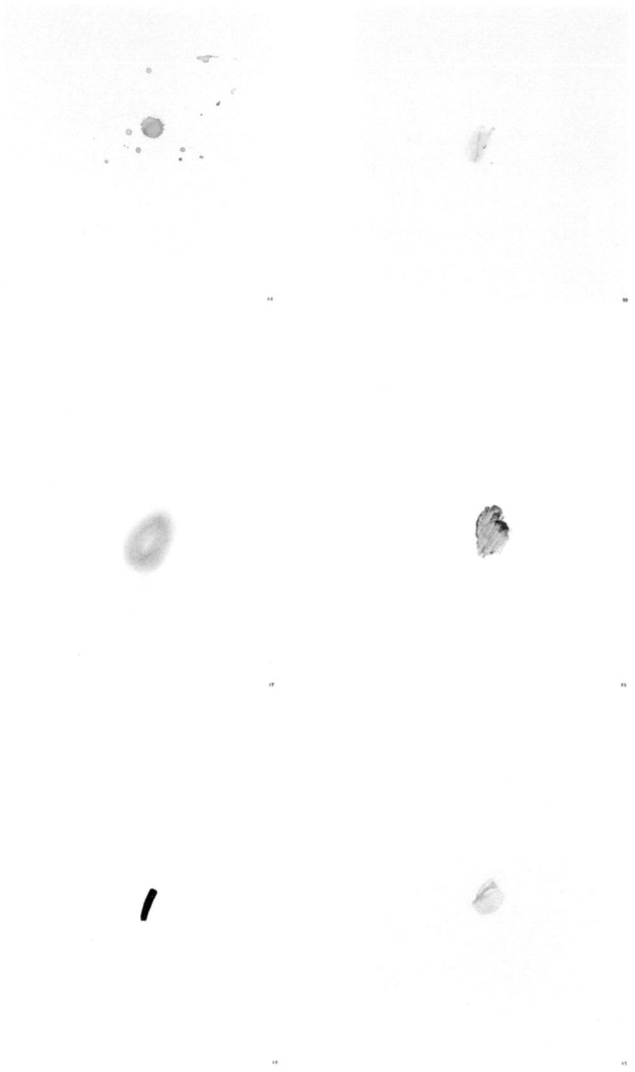

Cindy Sherman
(American, born 1954)
Untitled Film Still #21. 1978.
Gelatin silver print, 7½ × 9½ in.
(19.1 × 24.1 cm)
The Museum of Modern Art,
New York. Gift of Horace W.
Goldsmith Fund through Robert
B. Menschel
43

Cindy Sherman
(American, born 1954)
Untitled #197. 1989
Chromogenic color print,
31 5/16 × 20 7/8 in. (79.6 × 53.1 cm)
The Museum of Modern Art,
New York. Gift of The Family of
Man Fund
44

Cindy Sherman
(American, born 1954)
Untitled Film Still #13. 1978
Gelatin silver print, 9 7/16 × 7 ½ in.
(24 × 19.1 cm)
The Museum of Modern Art,
New York. Acquired through
the generosity of Jo Carole and
Ronald S. Lauder in memory of
Eugene M. Schwartz
44

Cindy Sherman
(American, born 1954)
Untitled Film Still #84. 1978
Gelatin silver print, 7½ × 9 7/16 in.
(19.1 × 24 cm)
The Museum of Modern Art,
New York. Purchase
44

Cindy Sherman
(American, born 1954)
Untitled #466. 2008
Chromogenic color print,
8 ft. 1 1/8 in. × 63 15/16 in.
(246.7 × 162.4 cm)
The Museum of Modern Art,
New York. Acquired through the
generosity of Robert B. Menschel
in honor of Jerry I. Speyer
45

Elizabeth Margulies

Elizabeth Margulies joined the Department of Education at The Museum of Modern Art in 1999. As Director of Family Programs and Initiatives, she develops and oversees gallery talks, workshops, artist talks, film programs, digital projects, and audio guides, as well as Art Lab, MoMA's interactive space for families. Before she came to MoMA, Liz was a teacher, and before that she studied clowning and performed across the country in giant spandex puppets. Now she clowns around with her son, Owen.

Liz and Cari have developed Art Making with MoMA kits and are the coauthors of "Make Art, Make Mistakes: A Creativity Sketchbook."

Cari Frisch

Cari Frisch started working in the Education Department at MoMA in 2005 and has simply never left. She develops activity guides, audio guides, and digital projects for kids, along with on-site programs for families, gallery conversations, art workshops, film screenings, and interactive spaces. Cari looks forward to sharing the projects in this book with her son, Bennett, when he is older.

Produced by the Department of Publications
The Museum of Modern Art, New York

Christopher Hudson, Publisher
Don McMahon, Editorial Director
Marc Sapir, Production Director

Edited by Emily Hall
Design, photography, prop and costume production by ALSO
Illustrations by Julia Rothman
Creative direction by Amanda Washburn
Young models photographed by Erin Holland and Leif Huron
Production by Hannah Kim
Printed and bound by Gorenjski Tisk Stortive, Slovenia

This book is typeset in Chivo and Louize.
The paper is 135 gsm Garda Matt.

Children's Book Working Group: Cerise Fontaine, Cari Frisch,
Samantha Friedman, Emily Hall, Hannah Kim, Elizabeth
Margulies, and Amanda Washburn

Young models and artists: Mungo Campbell, Eve Cohen,
Alexia Doroshenko, Fiona Kreizman, Henry Marks, Jason
Mats, Lina Pacheco, Maxine Paul-Emile, Genesis Solange
Pittman, Balthazar Plat, Violette Plat, Sophia Privine, Bella
Sibony, Lyric Sosin, Zephyr Sosin, Lucy Van Nostrand,
Oliver Van Nostrand, Ida Weills, Micah Wolfensohn, Karina
Zakabluk, Naomi Zola-Finlay, and Olive Zwicky

Poseidon costume by Gail Guerra

With thanks to Miranda Barry, Sara Bodinson, Michele
Carlucci, Isobel Cockerell, Jennifer Cohen, Liv Constable-
Maxwell, Jason Drimer, Naomi Falk, Paul Galloway, Lucy
Gallun, Stephen Gas, Judy Hecker, Lyn Hsieh, Dan Kaytes,
Chul R. Kim, Seok-Hee Lee, Jenna Madison, Cara Manes,
Tal Marks, Venus Morales-Pittman, Anne Morra, Matias
Pacheco, Greg Pittman, Emmanuel Plat, Rija Qureshi,
Larissa Raphael, Jennifer Small, Chay Costello Sosin, Sarah
Suzuki, Jess Van Nostrand, Adam Wolfensohn, Wendy
Woon, Gabrielle Zola, Calder Zwicky, and everyone who
has participated in MoMA's family programs over the years.

For more information, visit www.moma.org/family

© 2018 The Museum of Modern Art, New York

All rights reserved

Library of Congress Control Number: 2018948985
ISBN: 978-1-63345-037-0

Published by The Museum of Modern Art
11 West 53 Street
New York, New York 10019
www.moma.org

Distributed in the United States and Canada by Abrams
Books for Young Readers, an imprint of ABRAMS,
New York

Distributed outside the United States and Canada by
Thames & Hudson Ltd., London

Printed in Slovenia.